The Brown-Headed Parrot
a human's guide

by Marguerite Floyd

second edition

The African Brown-Headed Parrot
Copyright © 2012 by Marguerite Floyd

All rights reserved. No part of this publication may be reproduced, stored in or introduced into a retrieval system, or transmitted, in any form, or by any means (electronic, mechanical, photocopying, recording, or otherwise) without the written consent of the copyright owner.

Address inquires to
Cracked Seed Publishing
PO Box 11365
Lexington KY 40575
info@crackedseedpublishing.com

ISBN 978-0-9856075-0-0

Acknowledgements

A book such as this is not written in solitude. While my brown-headed parrot Charli has taught me much about the species, I also had a lot of help from people.

First thanks goes to Christy Catterton of Sassycast Aviary, in Woodbridge, Virginia, for her candor and suggestions. David Sternman of Out of Africa Aviaries in Louisville, Kentucky, also lent his expertise. Jerry Hamilton of Elizabethtown, Kentucky, was more than happy to give me his opinions from the viewpoint of his two brown-heads. And the wise folks on the Brown-Headed Parrot list on Yahoo Groups have added to my education for years

To all of these and their special brown-headed parrots, I thank you.

Table of Contents

Description 1

Why a Brown-Head? 4

Finding Your Special Brown-Head 6

Bringing Baby Home 11

Health & Diet 14

Communication 21

Grooming 22

Behavior 24

Other Matters 35

Good Foods 37

Everyday Common Behaviors 38

A Weekend Day in the Life of Charli 39

Continuing Your Education 42

DESCRIPTION

Sweet. Quiet. Plain. Charming. Mischievous. Jealous. Stubborn. All words used to describe the typical African brown-headed parrot.

Relatively rare both in the wild and in captivity, the brown-head is native to southern and eastern Africa – think Tanzania and Zanzibar. Brown-heads occupy mostly the plains, and frequently gather near rivers. They are shy both in the wild and in captivity.

Charli, the author's brown-head, as a five-month old.

Apart from gathering at rivers, brown-heads in the wild spend most of their time hidden in trees. They flock in groups of ten to fifteen individuals.

There are three accepted subspecies of brown-heads: *Poicephalus cryptoxanthus cryptoxanthus*, which are usually found in eastern Zululand to southern Mozambique; *Poicephalus c. tanganyikae*, which are found from the eastern coast of Kenya through southern Mozambique; and *Poicephalus c. zansibaricus*, which are found on the islands of Zanzibar and Pemba.

Physical Attributes
Visible differences between the subspecies are subtle, if visible at all.

Brown-headed parrots are about nine inches long, including a relatively short tail; larger than a cockatiel but a bit smaller than some conures. Their adult weight ranges from 96 to 130 grams, with 119-120 being the average.

The back and the top of the wings are dark green, while the rest of the body is a lighter green. Their toes are grayish and rough, with the nails being black.

Cryptoxanthus means "hidden yellow," which refers to the brilliant yellow underwings of the brown-head that you only see when the brown-head opens her wings or while in flight.

Their common name comes from the grayish brown feathers that cover the head and neck. The rest of the body is covered with green feathers of varied hues, many of them iridescent. This iridescence has led some breeders to call the species "emerald." The feathers above the feet are long and silky, often reaching the toes and looking like little short pants.

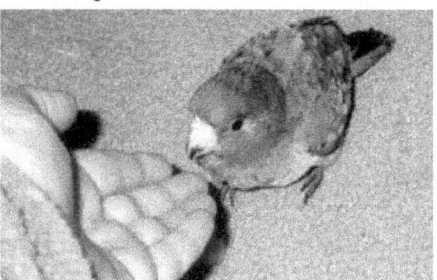

Charli, as a baby.

Brown-heads have very large and expressive eyes. As babies the eyes are big and round and dark. As they reach adulthood a grayish or yellowish gray ring appears around the iris; this ring is more pronounced in some birds than in others.

The beak is long and light gray with black on the upper mandible from the tip to about halfway up the beak. Some birds' lower beaks are black. Parrot beaks normally flake, so don't be alarmed if the beak looks dusty or as if it's peeling.

Brown-heads are not dimorphic, which means the only ways to be sure of the gender of your brown-head are DNA testing, surgical sexing, or the sudden appearance of an egg. Some breeders state that males weigh a bit more than females, but this isn't a hard and fast rule.

They are relatively long-lived; with good care they can live thirty years or more.

Charli as a three-year-old.

WHY A BROWN-HEAD?

Certainly other parrots boast more color, but a brown-head's personality, playfulness, and gleaming feathers more than make up for any perceived plainness. The reds and blues and yellows of other parrots are impressive, but the iridescence of a brown-head's green feathers has a rare beauty of its own.

Noise level is an important thing to consider if you live in an apartment or in a quiet neighborhood. The macaw call is designed to travel about five miles, which may not easily be tolerated by your neighbors.

The brown-head, on the other hand, has a quiet chirp, and even their cheerful screeches when playing are not as loud as the normal vocalizations of many larger parrots.

First Things First
Can you afford a roomy cage, a play stand, and a travel cage? Organic high-quality pellets, vegetables, and whole grains? Avian veterinary care, which can be expensive but is not optional? Toys your brown-head will destroy?

Do you have daily time to devote to your new friend? Not just having the bird on your shoulder while you watch television, but one-on-one time every day? Do you travel a lot? Do you know of a bird sitter, and can you afford one? If you have a spouse what is their opinion or willingness to having a parrot in the house? Are they willing to prepare the food or clean up after the brown-head?

Are there cats, dogs, reptiles, or other animals in your home? Are you sure you can protect your brown-head from them at all times? If you have other birds you cannot house your brown-head with them, so a new cage will be required.

Are you willing to give up your non-stick cookware and other items with non-stick coatings as well as scented candles, air fresheners, and scented cleaning products?

While this list may sound overly restrictive it is important that you realize what you're getting into with bringing home any parrot. If you cannot meet these requirements, save yourself and the brown-head a lot of grief (or even death) and wait until you're more prepared.

Compatibility with Children
Brown-heads are relatively calm birds and benefit from calm environments. Depending on the individual parrot, some enjoy the company of children while others will view children with dislike and attempt to drive them away. Children must be supervised around brown-heads, both for the safety of the child and the safety of the bird.

The natural high energy of children may make your brown-head nervous, so keep an eye on him, and keep him away from children if necessary.

Dangers
House plants can also pose dangers to your brown-head since he will insist on chewing everything his beak can reach. Some safe houses plants are ferns and palms, while poinsettia, holly, and philodendron are only a few of the plants known to be poisonous to parrots. This list is not inclusive so always check with your avian veterinarian or the breeder.

Heated non-stick cookware and appliances emit a chemical that can kill your brown-head. When I brought Charli, my brown-head, home I got rid of all my non-stick cookware. I now use stainless steel and cast iron, and I can honestly say I don't miss the non-stick cookware at all.

Charli supervises the drying of the dishes.

FINDING YOUR SPECIAL BROWN-HEAD

Adoption
Before you consider a breeder stop and consider adopting a brown-head that needs a new home. Often people must give up much-loved and cared for parrots for a variety of legitimate reasons, and brown-heads are no different. Often, too, brown-heads accidentally escape and become lost, ending up at a humane society or at a rescue organization.

These birds need good homes and can be just as loveable and wonderful as baby brown-heads.

Breeders
If you decide to purchase a brown-headed parrot from a breeder, here are some tips to help you find a good breeder.

Ask other brown-head owners. If they purchased their brown-head from a breeder, was the baby trusting of humans, in good health, properly weaned?

Does the breeder offer any assurance, such as a return policy if the bird is found ill by an avian veterinarian within the first 48 or 72 hours of ownership?

Are you allowed to visit the breeder and see the babies? Are the facilities clean? Many breeders will not allow you to see the parents since brown-heads are shy breeders and there is always a chance you might unknowingly bring in a disease, so having a "closed" operation is perfectly legitimate.

Does the breeder answer your questions completely and respectfully? Is the breeder willing to provide references?

Does the breeder seem to be interviewing you instead of you interviewing them? Be completely honest with your answers; good breeders want their babies to go to excellent homes, and many will refuse to sell a baby if they don't believe you will provide an optimal environment. Some breeders will even suggest a different species depending on the type of questions you ask and your individual circumstances and environment.

Ask the breeder who their avian veterinarian is; if the breeder does not have an avian veterinarian you can't be sure the flock is healthy.

Are the baby brown-heads active and playing, with bright dark eyes? Are they comfortable with gentle handling? Are they accustomed to usual household noises such as televisions or vacuum cleaners?

Is the baby fully weaned; that is, consistently eating on her own? Is she eating a varied diet, including fruits, vegetables, and grains? A brown-head baby that's already eating a varied diet will be more willing to try new foods when she gets to your home.

Is the baby fully fledged; that is, has she been allowed to fly for at least three to four weeks? The longer she has been weaned and fledged, the better for both of you.

Good breeders will encourage you to keep in touch once your new friend is in her new home, and will be willing to answer questions once you and the bird have settled in.

Cage Issues
When it comes to cages, bigger is better. In addition to room for toys, dishes, and perches your brown-head's cage must be large enough so that she can spread and flap her wings, run back and forth, hang upside down, and climb around. The cage should be at the bare *minimum* 18X18X24 *if* you plan to have your brown-head out of her cage a lot; otherwise, the cage should be larger. Bar spacing of half an inch to an inch is acceptable; too large a space may allow your brown-head to get her head caught between the bars.

Safe cages are stainless steel or powder coated. Avoid brass, copper, zinc, or galvanized cages since these surfaces are toxic if/when your brown-head chews on them. Also avoid wooden cages, since your brown-head will simply chew through the wood.

A basic rectangle shaped cage is best. Parrots tend to not be comfortable in circular cages, and fancy shapes may lessen the available space your brown-head has in which to move and play.

A good cage is your bird's home and refuge; it is not a prison.

Make things easy on yourself and get a cage with a removable grate and removable tray that sits beneath the grate. This will make cleaning so much easier. A large door on the front of the cage will also allow you to easily get inside to clean more thoroughly.

You don't have to buy special liners; newspaper will do just fine. In fact, it is recommended that you avoid any type of bedding since it can encourage mold and bacteria growth. Newspaper, on the other hand, is cheap and allows you to monitor your brown-head's droppings.

Because brown-heads are so shy, most of them appreciate a place to hide in their cages. This can be as simple as a towel draped over a corner of the cage or a cozy sleeping tent.

A variety of perches is essential. Since birds spend all their time on their feet, they require perches of different shapes, materials, and diameters. A good basic width allows your brown-head to wrap her toes half or three-quarters around the perch, with smaller and larger diameters also available.

Good materials for perches are very tightly woven rope, and clean untreated branches from safe trees such as apple.

Play Stands & Travel Cages

Your brown-head needs a change of scenery just as you do, so a portable play stand can provide that. Have your bird on her play stand near you while you work on your computer or talk on the phone. A good play stand has cups for water and food and room for toys to ward off boredom.

A travel cage is a good investment since you'll need a way to transport your bird to the veterinarian's or just to go for nice rides in the car. Again, the cage should have cups for water and food and room for a toy or two.

Cleaning

Having a brown-head, or any parrot, share your home requires different ways of thinking about cleanliness. Change the paper in the cage every day. Change the water every day or more often if your brown-head insists on dunking his food in his dishes. You can easily wipe down the cage every day with a very weak solution of vinegar and water, or you can purchase such bird-safe cleaners as Poop-Off. Periodically, you'll want to do a thorough cleaning, including dismantling the cage. I find that a steam vapor cleaner is perfect for this type of cleaning since it doesn't require any chemicals. Never leave your parrot inside the cage while using a steam cleaner or power washer to clean the cage.

Throw the toys and perches in the dishwasher along with the food and water dishes – if the toys or perches are dishwasher safe, of course.

Your brown-head is very sensitive to chemicals, so only use cleansers that are bird safe. If you're not sure about a product, don't use it. Ask your parrot-owning friends what they recommend, or visit some of the bird stores on the Internet.

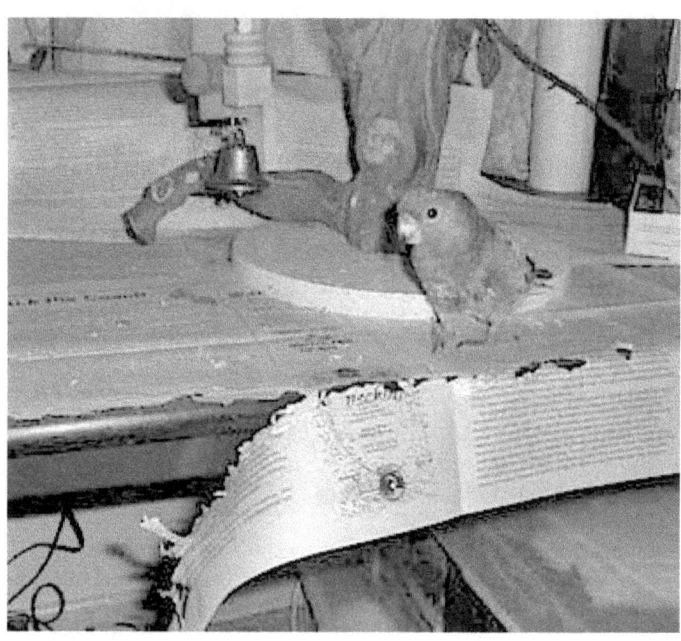

Charli is proud of her paper-chewing skills.

BRINGING BABY HOME

You will, of course, already have your new friend's cage set up before bringing her home. You should do all you can to lessen any stress on the bird during the move.

An avian veterinarian visit is highly recommended as soon as you get your brown-head. Your avian veterinarian can check the condition of your new friend, get a good baseline on her health in case there's an emergency or change in health, and give you advice on diet and behavior. You will also want to have the bird tested for the more common diseases, especially if you are adopting.

Some babies will food regress due to the stress of moving to a new home and being in quarantine. Have the breeder show you how to feed your baby his formula for that first day or so in case he does food regress. Some babies will also ignore food they don't recognize, so feed your baby what the breeder has been feeding.

If there are other birds in your home, you must quarantine your new bird for a minimum of 30 days. Often the stress of moving to a new home will bring out latent conditions; hence the need for quarantine. This 30 days is usually enough time for any symptoms of contagious diseases to appear, and can protect your other birds.

Quarantine is done by putting your brown-head in a room separate from your other birds. It is all right if your birds hear one another, so soundproofing isn't necessary.

Remember that many avian diseases are spread through contact with hands and clothes, so visit your quarantined brown-head after you've visited your regular flock. This will minimize spreading any diseases via your clothing. Once you've visited your brown-head, change your clothes and shoes before going back to your regular flock. Wash those clothes before wearing them to handle your regular flock.

Quarantine may seem like a lot of work, especially if your brown-head looks healthy, but it is worth any amount of inconvenience to spare yourself the heartbreak of losing a bird to a contagious disease.

If your house is a comfortable temperature for you, it's probably comfortable for your brown-head. While brown-heads are native to Africa, they are fine with consistent temperatures in the ranges of temperatures we enjoy.

Your brown-head may be frightened and wary of her new surroundings at first, maybe even refusing to eat. Don't attempt to force her to come out of her cage or socialize until she's more comfortable. Try sitting beside her cage and reading to her or just talking softly. Let her watch you go about your daily routines.

Attention
There is a belief in the parrot world that if you give a baby parrot too much attention he will grow up to expect that much, or more, attention. Actually, it's not so much the amount of time you spend with a baby parrot as the quality of that time.

It's natural for us to want to play with our new friend and to admire her every chance we get. Where some owners get into trouble, however, is in not providing interactive opportunities for the bird to learn to play and amuse herself independently. Most of us have jobs outside the home and aren't able to stay home with the parrot all the time. It's important to encourage the bird to play with her toys without you, and for you to provide suitable toys and foraging opportunities to keep her occupied.

By encouraging your brown-head to play with toys and entertain herself, you are helping develop a healthy parrot and a healthy relationship with your parrot.

What's a "normal" amount of time or attention for a brown-head? Ideally, every parrot seems to require direct,

The African Brown-Headed Parrot 13

one-on-one attention every day; at a minimum of fifteen to thirty minutes a day.

If you cannot provide that direct attention each day, try to increase that attention on those days you have more time. They also benefit from more ambient attention, such as watching your activities from a play gym or watching television perched on your lap. Parrots cannot thrive being left in their cages and admired from afar. They are highly intelligent creatures and need much social interaction.

Charli always thinks it's time to play instead of work.

HEALTH & DIET

Brown-heads are usually hale and healthy, especially those from good breeders. Of course, much depends on good nutrition and a healthy environment.

Your brown-head should have regular annual well-bird visits with an avian veterinarian. At this visit the avian veterinarian may take small blood samples and a sample of droppings to examine for parasites and disease. The avian veterinarian will also listen to the bird's lung sounds, and examine the eyes and ears and throat.

Some birds do fine at the vet; others hate it. Just the way people feel about doctors.

Don't worry about your brown-head not trusting you after a visit to the vet; he'll most likely blame the vet and not you. Like being held in a towel, he'll blame the towel, not the human.

The veterinarian visit will be a good chance to let your brown-head see you as the "rescuer" who saved him from the scary person in the white coat.

Ask, ask, ask the avian vet anything. Ask what the vet's doing and why if you don't understand something. Ask the vet to demonstrate the best way to teach behaviors, such as step-ups. Find out what recommended lab tests will show and how much they'll cost you. It's good for you to know what's going on, and the avian vet will see you as someone who is a good parrot owner.

If money is an issue, discuss it with your veterinarian. You probably have more financial options than you realize.

If the vet refuses to answer your questions or makes you feel you're wasting his time, find another avian vet.

Remember that not all veterinarians are avian veterinarians. An avian veterinarian is one who sees primarily exotic birds and continues to educate herself with the latest avian research and techniques. Ask your parrot-owning friends or the breeder for recommendations.

Now is the time to find an avian veterinarian and develop a relationship with her. A baseline of weight and blood values can help the veterinarian more easily provide care if your brown-head is ill or needs emergency care. Trying to find an avian veterinarian when your bird is sick can cost your brown-head critical time he may not have.

Charli shows off her normal adult weight.

Now is also a good time to purchase a gram scale. An inexpensive dietary gram scale will do as well as the more expensive models. Weigh your brown-head after his morning poop every day for several weeks, and record the daily weights. Then weigh him once or twice a week for another month or so, and then once or a twice a month for the rest of his life or if you suspect he isn't feeling well.

A good baseline of his weight will help alert you to possible illnesses. In fact, the first signal of an illness may be a weight loss.

Illness
Like all flock animals, parrots will hide their illness or injury as long as they can. There are subtle signs your brown-head may not feel well, but they require that you have watched her carefully and can recognize behavior that isn't quite "right." Sleeping more, not eating quite as much, spending more time on the cage floor, undigested food in the droppings, a change in communication, discharge from the beak or vent can all be signs of a problem.

If your brown-head is sitting on the cage floor, fluffed up, "depressed," eyes closed but head not turned to the back your bird is so ill he cannot hide it any longer and needs to be seen by an avian veterinarian immediately.

While brown-heads are not known to be as susceptible to feather destruction as some species of parrot, it is still a possibility. Feather destructive behavior can be caused by numerous conditions or situations. If your brown-head begins destroying her feathers a visit to an avian veterinarian is your first move. Are there things in the environment that may be upsetting to your brown-head, from his point of view? Is he getting enough sleep? He may be allergic to a dye or additive in the pellets you're providing; he may need a tiny bit of red palm oil added to his diet.

It's also a good idea to work with a parrot behavior consultant as soon as you notice your brown-head is destroying his feathers. A consultant can help you identify things that might be contributing to the problem and help you design an optimum environment for your brown-head.

Diet
In the wild, brown-heads eat two main meals a day; one in the morning and one in the evening before roosting.

Brown-heads in the wild eat seeds, nuts, fruits, grains, and flowers. Captive brown-heads seem susceptible to fatty liver disease. In the wild, brown-heads eat a high carbohydrate diet with higher levels of protein and fat in the breeding season.

Feed fresh food, organic when possible. If you wouldn't eat it don't feed it to your bird.

Your brown-head may be suspicious of new foods. He may examine it first with one eye and then the other, and still not approach it. If your brown-head is turning up his beak at a particular food, try eating it in front of him. Make a lot of enthusiastic noises and act like you want it all for yourself and won't share. After a few tries, he may decide to try it. Parrots are flock animals and love eating with their humans. If he still refuses, keep trying. Sometimes a brown-head will avoid a food for weeks or months, then one day decide it's the most delicious thing in the world.

Because we still do not know the exact nutritional requirements for parrots, many parrots benefit from an organic pelleted diet. Pellets are formulated so that each one contains the same nutrients as all the others with the nutrients we do know are necessary. Avoid pellets with artificial ingredients or dyes.

Most brown-heads enjoy fruits such as oranges, lemons, and kiwi and berries such as blueberries, raspberries, and strawberries.

Vegetables, especially fresh ones, are also a necessary part of the brown-head's diet. A stalk of broccoli or slices of apples on a skewer can serve as a forging opportunity while you're at work or out shopping. Brown-heads enjoy cooked or raw peas, green beans, squash, legumes, carrots, sprouted seeds, romaine lettuce, cooked egg, kale, peppers, corn, and sweet potatoes. They also like pasta and rice.

Grains such as millet and oats are also part of a healthy brown-head diet.

Nuts and seeds, while favored by brown-heads, make good treats since they contain too much fat to be a regular part of their diet. Almonds, walnuts, peanuts, and pine nuts are favorites. Cheerios and shredded wheat also make good treats in small amounts.

Like us, brown-heads can get tired of the same foods day after day, which is another reason dietary variety is so important.

Brown-heads tend to love human junk food – chips, nachos, etc. These should be very limited, given only as small, special treats. And remember that what we consider a small amount is most likely huge for a small bird.

Your brown-head will often hold larger pieces of food in her left foot. She will take a small bite, and then either drop the rest of the food on the floor, or take another bite and let that fall to the floor.

This is a natural behavior of parrots; the theory is that by dropping so much of their food parrots are keeping the rainforests fertile and feeding the creatures that live on the ground.

For us humans, it just means we get to clean up more.

Keep offering foods in different forms. For example, some brown-heads like raw carrots cut into small pieces, others want the whole carrot to chew on, while still others will only eat carrots if they're cooked and mashed.

Try a pre-mixed food made with grains and vegetables with rice or pasta. You can sneak a few more vegetables into those as well.

Poop
You'll want to become acquainted with your brown-head's normal droppings, since abnormal droppings can signal an illness.

Normal parrot poop is composed of three parts: urine, urate (white matter), and feces (green).

Some foods such as berries may color the poop and is no cause for alarm, but a change that lasts more than 24 hours calls for a visit to the avian veterinarian.

The first morning poop will tend to be much larger than poops the rest of the day.

Sleep
Like all parrots, brown heads require 10 to 12 hours of quiet, dark sleep a night. Many brown-heads enjoy a special covered area for sleeping, such as a Hide 'n Sleep. Please note that your brown-head may chew the fabric or the hanger until it's just right to him, so snip off any stray threads to avoid your bird becoming entangled. Check periodically that the threads or elastic are not frayed.

Most brown-heads sleep with their heads turned back and tucked into their neck feathers, with one foot drawn up into the belly. Some owners, however, report that their brown-head sleeps with head and tail straight, with the body as high to the top of the cage or sleep enclosure as possible. Other brown-heads are happy sleeping on a favorite perch.

Often, Charli will curl up on the cage floor for a nap, turn her head back and stare at me with one large dark eye while her head is tucked into her back feathers -- a coy expression meant to elicit more admiration.

Many owners find their brown-heads benefit from a special smaller sleep cage that is placed in another, more quiet room. Such a cage should have food and water available but basically be used only for sleeping. During the day the bird is placed in his regular cage or play stand.

Molting
Molting is the process of losing old feathers and replacing them with new feathers. Some brown-heads molt once a year, while others seem to molt a little every day. Many

brown-heads are irritable during this process, so be patient with them.

When a new feather comes in it is wrapped in a keratin sheath, which helps push out the old feather. The shaft of the new feather is filled with blood and nerves and is very sensitive. If you touch one of these blood feathers expect a sharp reprimand from your brown-head. As the feather unfurls the blood supply ebbs away and so do the nerve endings.

New feathers are prickly to your brown-head, so gentle extra scratches are appreciated during this time. Extra baths help, too.

Charli after a bath.

COMMUNICATION

Most brown-heads are capable of human speech, but not that many take up that form of communication. They are marvelous mimics, and any reinforcement you give them for sounds are more likely to be repeated. Some owners believe that males tend to talk more than females.

Sounds
While brown-heads are relatively quiet (no parrot is quiet all the time) they do have a repertoire of sounds. You may hear "kreek" or "meep" when she is happy and feeling loving and content.

Early evening squawks are normal sounds for brown-heads; they may last three to seven or so minutes.

When your brown-head is sleepy and content and relaxed, you may hear a grinding noise. This comes from her grinding her beak. Most people enjoy this sound since it does indicates a happy parrot.

A growl indicates she is afraid or alarmed about something. Back off, find whatever it is that's frightening her and remove it.

Remember that any sound you make a fuss over will be repeated. If your brown-head is screaming about something, talk softly to him while you check out the environment. There may be something alarming next to the cage or staring in the window.

If the screaming continues, be sure your brown-head hasn't injured himself. Wait until he's quiet, even for a few seconds, and then praise him for being quiet. Make it a big deal, but only when he's being quiet.

Praise your brown-head any time she's being quiet, playing with her toys, or being particularly adorable.

GROOMING

The nails of a brown-head are extremely sharp, and your brown-head will insist that they stay that way. After even a very gentle trimming of the nails, a brown-head can easily lose balance because the sharpness is so crucial to her grip.

Encouraging your brown-head to use a sandy perch (not a concrete one) can help blunt the nails just enough to prevent scratching your skin, though some owners say even this doesn't work.

When you have your brown-head's nails blunted, be prepared for him to do some sulking and to spend a lot of time resharpening the nails with his beak.

Play with your brown-head's toes, if she'll allow it, so that nail trimming won't be such a dramatic affair for either of you.

Charli is very possessive and protective of her body. No one touches her toes, though quick and brief strokes to her wings are tolerated. Just barely. Other brown-heads, however, are very cuddly.

Bathing

Many breeders don't bathe baby brown-heads, so it's up to the new owner to offer the brown-head the opportunity to experience the joys of water.

Don't expect this to happen immediately. In fact, it took nearly two years before my brown-head became tolerant of bathing. She still isn't convinced it's fun, but she will hold still for it now.

Many brown-heads prefer to bathe in a shallow dish of water or by being misted with a fine spray of water. Experiment to find the most preferred method, and keep trying. Place a shallow dish of water in the cage and pretend to ignore your brown-head while she checks it out. She may only get her chest wet, but that's all right. When she splashes herself in the water, be sure to give her lots and lots of praise.

If she fluffs her feathers happily under mist from a spray bottle, give her lots of praise for that, too. You want her to associate bathing with fun.

Trimming Wing Feathers
A gentle wing trim will allow your brown-head to fly but not gain altitude. I keep Charli's wings trimmed to lessen the chance of her accidentally flying out the door or flying into a window.

Have your avian veterinarian show you how to correctly trim the wing feathers. The trim should be symmetrical and not cut into blood feathers. There are no nerves in fully formed feather sheathes, so there is no pain when trimming mature feathers.

While many people believe it is more natural to leave their brown-heads fully feathered, keep in mind that our homes are not natural habitats for parrots and it is up to us to keep them safe.

Charli enjoys chewing up this foraging box that has almonds hidden inside.

BEHAVIOR

Step-Ups

One of the most important things you can teach your brown-head is how to step up. Step-ups will help you work with your brown-head and can help calm him when he's being contrary due to hormones or just a bad mood.

With your brown-head on a flat surface or your finger, gently press your index finger against his lower belly, above his legs. He should automatically step up onto your finger. As soon as one foot is on your finger, say "Step up!" Lavishly praise him for his accomplishment. Repeat this five or six times, saying "step up" each time, praising loudly and enthusiastically each time.

A good time to start step-ups is right now. And later in the day. Then for a few minutes in the afternoon. And, of course, early in the evening. Always stop before your bird gets tired, while it's still fun.

When stepping up becomes automatic, practice "laddering" a few times a week. Laddering is simply using first one index finger and then the other so that the bird is "climbing" onto your fingers as if on a ladder.

Say "step up" each time you ask your bird to step up onto your hand; it should become automatic for both of you.

Body Language

Learning and reading your brown-head's body language will go a long way in developing a good relationship.

When relaxed and at ease, a brown-head will sit with her feathers loose; not fluffed up or tight against her body. She will be alert and watch you and her surroundings with interest. She will preen a lot, so much so that you may wonder if she has fleas.

Rapid opening and closing of beak with relaxed feathers usually means the brown-head is being friendly. Feel free to return the body language to show you want to be friends, too.

Feathers held tight to the body can indicate fear or a warning. This can often be accompanied by the slightest lift of the wings in case flight is necessary.

When your brown-head is angry with you, he'll most likely turn his back to you. When this happens, just give him some time. Soon he'll have forgiven you and be willing to be friends again.

Sticking the tongue out slightly to the side of the beak usually indicates the end of a behavior and/or satisfaction.

Many brown-heads exhibit what some owners call "shadow boxing." This is a twisting, writhing, snake-like motion that's generally meant to warn you off. If you ignore this, be prepared for a bite.

Watching the eyes of your brown-head can cue you as to her mood. Wide, round eyes mean she's alert and curious. Slight narrowing of the eyes means she's getting angry or warning you to behave.

Contact Call

Flock animals keep in touch with one another, even when they're out of sight. Your brown-head considers you as part of his flock, and he'll expect you to keep in touch, too.

Periodically, your brown-head will chirp if left alone. Call softly back to let him know that even though he can't see you all is well and everyone in the flock is safe.

Ignoring contact calls can lead to screaming, which can be a difficult problem to solve.

Screaming and Biting

Brown-heads are known for being relatively quiet, compared with other parrots. But your brown-head can and will scream on occasion. Loud calls in the early evening and in the mornings are normal behavior, and last for perhaps three to seven minutes. If you do not reinforce this behavior it will not escalate into screaming. However, it is a natural behavior and cannot be changed.

Most brown-heads would prefer not to bite you, and will often bite because you have ignored the warning signs. There are times your brown-head may not want to be petted and will pull away from your hand. If you persist, you're setting yourself up for a nip. If you still continue, you may receive a harder bite. This teaches your brown-head that you won't take a gentle nip as a warning and will only respond with a bite, which he will deliver the next time instead of a warning.

Acting dramatically and/or yelling will be perceived by your brown-head as a reward for biting. Being rewarded for a behavior increases the likelihood that it will be repeated. If you are bitten, just frown at your brown-head and turn away.

If your brown-head seems "wound up," put her down or back in her cage until she calms down so as to not escalate into biting. This will probably only take a few minutes.

Never allow your brown-head on your shoulder if he is acting the least bit naughty or jealous. You cannot read his body language while he is on your shoulder, and it is too easy to suffer a facial bite from a parrot on your shoulder.

Jealousy
Brown-heads are notoriously territorial and jealous. To use the telephone with a brown-head perched on your shoulder or lap is to invite a bite. I have learned to put Charli either back in her cage or on my knee when I have to be on the phone. She gives me dirty looks but is far enough away to not bite me or attack the phone.

Even allowing your brown-head on the same surface as your keyboard may result in nips to your fingers since it's obvious you're paying more attention to the keyboard than to your bird.

This jealously applies especially to other birds in the household, as well as children and other animals. This seems to be instinctual, so having your brown-head out and unattended can end in disaster. The brown-head is quick and determined. Even if you're watching, the brown-head can strike suddenly, before you can react. *Always* keep a very safe distance between your brown-head and other birds and animals. Don't allow your brown-head to wander around the house unsupervised.

Those times your brown-head becomes overly possessive of his cage, remove all the toys and dishes, and then replace them with different toys and dishes. Or just move everything around in the cage. This is usually just upsetting enough to stop possessive behavior. For a while.

A brown-head can decide he loves one person in the household above all others, and could be very determined not to have anyone else around when the loved one is near. To avoid this, expose the brown-head to lots of people; if she's afraid or reluctant, let her watch your interactions from the safety of her cage.

Ego
Your position as a human on this planet is to pamper and pet your brown-headed parrot. At least, this is how brown-heads appear to think. Idle hands and fingers should be put to use stroking head feathers and rubbing under chins. I have never heard of a brown-headed parrot that got tired of petting. Ever.

Discipline
Parrots do not understand discipline as humans define it. Hitting your brown-head will only cause him to mistrust you; he will not associate his behavior with the consequence of being physically attacked.

Brown-heads do, however, understand when you give them a dirty look and turn your back to them. This needs to be done immediately upon unacceptable behavior. Often, being put back in his cage briefly to calm down is an effective form of discipline.

Remember that any behavior you reinforce with attention or laughter or even yelling and fussing will more likely be repeated in an effort to have you repeat your behavior.

Chewing
Like all parrots, brown-heads have a talent for chewing. The beak of a parrot is full of nerves and some owners believe that chewing simply feels good to the parrot. It is widely believed that chewing helps keep the beak to its proper size and shape, which is essential for eating.

The beak of the brown-head is a marvelous tool. Not only can it crack some soft-shelled nuts and splinter all manner of wooden toys, it can also dismantle your furniture. A year or so ago I bought a nice expensive adjustable office chair. I assembled it carefully, and when I was finished I tapped in the screw head covers that are permanent once they've been installed.

It took Charli about ten minutes to get each of the screw head covers off and maybe another five minutes to loosen each bolt. It's only a matter of time before the entire chair collapses under me, since Charli insists on loosening each bolt whenever I tighten them.

Another favorite toy of Charli's is the top of felt tip pens, the ones you can't remove. It takes her a few seconds to pry it off with her beak, then we play tug o war so I can get it back. As a sly maneuver she'll hold onto the top and then bow her head, which means I'm supposed to pet her and presumably forget about the pen top. Sometimes I do.

Your brown-head is a chewing machine. Accept it now. He will chew his toys to splinters, he will chew your tee-shirts and jeans or more expensive clothing, he will happily snap off the buttons on your blouses, he will chew your tax return and homework, the couch, the cords to and from your computer, the buttons on the remote – anything that can be reached with his beak is fair game.

Your brown-head will be happy to chew up all of your papers, too.

Knowing this, it is your responsibility to direct that chewing toward acceptable items. Electrical cords are not acceptable chew toys, but a piece of rolled up newspaper is.

Because your brown-head will not see any differences between your new clothing and your old clothing it's up to you to control access to your clothing. Old tee shirts can withstand a few holes and the occasional deposit of poop, and old work shirts can withstand having their buttons chewed off, but keep your brown-head away from your new designer suit.

My brown-head's most favorite chewing object is a simple roll of new adding machine tape. I stick a toy pencil through the hole of the tape, wedge it between the bars, and she happily chews on that paper for days. Your brown-head may prefer a hanging wooden toy or Shredders. Offer choices.

Don't forget that he may become bored with a toy, so offer different toys. Toys should be rotated on a regular basis to help your brown-head avoid boredom.

Foraging
Parrots spend much of their in the wild foraging for food. They are designed to expend large amounts of energy finding food. When we bring them into our homes, put their food and water in front of them, and then leave them alone for most of the day, that energy has nowhere to go. This can lead to feather destructive behavior, biting, and screaming.

A skewer and a carousel are good foraging toys.

Providing foraging opportunities for your brown-head can be as simple as putting fresh fruits and vegetables on a skewer, and hanging the skewer in the middle of the cage, just out of easy reach. Numerous toys are available that can hold nuts and other treats that can only be released with some thinking and effort on your brown-head's part. I frequently put partially cracked almonds in the shell in a plastic carousel-type toy hung in the middle of the cage. This requires Charli to reach far out from her perch. She then has to keep the toy still while she works at chewing the rest of the shell and eating the nut inside. When I get home from work all the almonds have been eaten, and she's quite pleased with herself.

Make your brown-head's foraging opportunities challenging but not impossible. The brown-head's beak cannot crack open almond or walnut shells, and a toy that is too difficult to manipulate may frustrate your brown-head.

Start with something simple. Let him watch you place his favorite treat in a bowl and then place a clean paper towel over the bowl. He will have to remove the paper towel to get to the treat. You may have to coach him through it the first couple of times.

Night Frights

Poicephalus seem to be more prone to panic and to night frights than many other parrots. Seeing a brown-head freeze from fear is disturbing and requires time and patience to help her recover.

We're not always sure what causes the panic attacks; poicephalus usually don't see well in the dark so they may be responding to the sound of a mouse, or changing light and shadow from passing traffic, or maybe even a bad dream.

When these frights happen at night, there will be a rustle in the cage and then silence. When you turn on the light and lift the cover, your brown-head will be frozen to the perch, his feathers slicked down tight, eyes wide, and body tense.

Talk softly to him and keep reassuring him that all is well. If possible, stroke his feathers gently. Don't try to pry him off the perch or remove him from his cage. Remain calm, and explain that whatever frightened him is gone now (assuming it is). Be patient. It can literally take hours for a brown-head to loosen his grip on that perch and resume his normal activities.

Panic attacks during the day follow much the same pattern, though you have a better opportunity to stop them if you're present. A sudden loud knock on the door or the screech of a fire truck going by may trigger the response in your brown-head, but if you immediately reassure your bird and keep your body language and manner calm, your brown-head will feel more secure.

Don't ignore night frights or panic behavior; it could develop into phobic behavior, which is much more difficult to deal with for both you and your brown-head.

The Invisible Brown-Head
One afternoon I had some workers doing some outdoor painting. When the job was finished they came inside and closed the door behind them. The glass doors to the deck were open but the screen was securely in place.

My brown-head had been inside her cage with the cage door open so I didn't pay much attention to her whereabouts while I wrote a check for the work. Then I glanced at the cage and didn't see her. I didn't see her anywhere.

I called to her and got silence. All the workers looked around the room while I went through the living room looking and calling. After a few minutes, panic growing in my throat, one of the workers pointed to the top of the cage.

There she was, sitting perfectly still and perfectly blended into the background, even though her colors were in contrast to the background. We had all looked inside the cage and on top of the cage and beside the cage and had not seen her.

She has done this several times, and I am always astonished at how still and "invisible" she can make herself. When I find her she always has an expression on her face as if I'm a sucker who fell for it again. Other owners have reported the same thing. It's an unnerving experience.

In the wild, baby brown-heads gather in "neighborhoods" in trees and dense foliage and remain perfectly motionless while their parents gather food. They do not move until the parents return. This may account for the ability to remain so motionless the brown-head becomes invisible.

Regurgitation
When your brown-head loves you and wants to show his deep affection, he may regurgitate. Humans are not overly impressed with this, but it is a sign of great love for parrots. Just gently distract him and ignore the behavior.

Fun
Most brown-heads love hanging upside down and will do so frequently. Many brown-heads enjoy hanging by one toe from a swing or rope perch and screeching as they swing themselves around. I always have to check when Charli does this, just in case she's gotten herself entangled in something.

At least once a week I will have Charli sit on my finger, ask her if she's ready, then run through the hallway into the study and back. Most of the time Charli will flap her wings hard while gripping my fingers. We'll repeat this a couple of times until she's a little winded. It's a good workout for her (and me, too).

It's also a good idea to play more physical games such as Fetch, Soccer, Wrestle The Parrot, or Keep Away. These games, while gentle, can provide a good workout for your brown-head, as well as create a closer bond between you.

When your brown-head is particularly pleased with herself she may wag her tail very quickly. This is what Mattie Sue

Athan calls a "happiness behavior." My brown-head often does this when she thinks she's manipulated me into petting her.

Brown-heads are very intelligent, and yours may enjoy learning tricks. Using positive reinforcement can make it easy to teach her such tricks as spreading and hold out her wings like an eagle, or turning around on cue.

One of Charli's favorite games is Blink. Charli blinks at me, and I blink back. This game can go on for as long as ten minutes, with some blinks at frequent intervals and some at not so frequent intervals.

Nearly all parrots enjoy a good session of I'll Drop It and You Pick It Up. This game is exactly what it sounds like; your brown-head will drop an object and you will pick it up and return it to her. Whereupon she'll drop it again, and you'll be expected to pick it up again.

Be creative in playing with your bird. Parrots love to play and have fun; let them show you how.

OTHER MATTERS

Breeding
Brown-heads tend to be shy breeders.

In the wild, brown-heads nest in tree cavities, generally facing north. In captivity, your brown-heads will appreciate L-shaped nest boxes.

Some brown-heads lay only one clutch in the winter; other brown-heads lay several clutches throughout the year. A normal clutch is two to four eggs, laid at two-day intervals. Incubation is approximately 26 days, with weaning taking place at about ten weeks.

Brown-heads reach puberty from two to three years of age, though they are usually four years of age before laying fertile eggs. During this time females exhibit the "skirt dance," which is a breeding pose. It consists of the brown-head standing low to the ground, giving soft chirps, and slowly turning in a circle. During these times do not encourage your brown-head; ignore the behavior and your brown-head will soon return to her normal behaviors.

Stroking a parrot's wings, under the wings, or down the back can trigger sexual responses, so keep your petting to your brown-head's head, face, and neck.

Escape
Get in the habit now of keeping doors and windows closed. Be sure your window screens are secure. Anything could startle your brown-head, causing her to fly across a room and out an open door.

Now is an excellent time to take a picture of your brown-head, just in case you need to create a flyer in a hurry.

Microchip your bird. This is the only way to legally prove you own your bird. A tiny chip is embedded in the bird's breast. It's inexpensive and doesn't hurt the bird. In fact, all of my birds are microchipped, and they fussed more over the alcohol swab than the injection.

Most humane societies and veterinarians have scanners that can easily detect the presence of a microchip. When a chip is detected the person scanning can contact a central number, which will provide the owner's name and contact information.

If your bird does escape, DON'T PANIC. Your bird is probably frightened enough for both of you, so remain calm.

Put her cage in the yard with her favorite treats and water. If she has a mate, bring the mate out in his cage.

Keep her in sight as long as you can. Talk to her.

Put up flyers everywhere. Contact pet stores, veterinarian offices, the post office, and the fire and police departments. Offer a reward, especially to children in your neighborhood. Post on www.911parrotalert.com and www.birdhotline.com.

DON'T give up! Birds are often found weeks, months, even years later, near home and even several states away.

Multiple Birds

You may wonder if your long brown-head is lonely and would benefit from another brown-head or a parrot of another species. Brown-heads tend to be very jealous and intolerant of other species and often of other brown-heads. A brown-head can be kept happily as a single bird.

Charli has to be watched when she's out at the same time my cockatiels are out.

GOOD FOODS

This list is by no means complete, but it'll give you a good start

Vegetables
Apples
Broccoli
Carrots
Cooked Egg
Corn
Green Beans
Kale
Legumes
Peas
Peppers
Romaine
Sprouted Seeds
Squash
Sweet Potatoes

Fruits
Kiwi
Lemons
Limes
Oranges

Berries
Blackberries
Blueberries
Raspberries
Strawberries

Grains
Flax Seed
Millet
Oatmeal

Do Not Feed
Alcohol
Avocado
Caffeine
Chocolate

Charli approves of this mix of fresh vegetables and grains.

Occasional Treats
Almonds
Grapes
Pine Nuts
Peanuts
Walnuts
Shredded wehat
Cheerios

EVERYDAY COMMON BEHAVIORS

Your brown-head will most likely do all of these every day or so. They are all perfectly normal behaviors.

Preen (no, your brown-head does not have fleas).
Molt.
Chew anything within reach.
Scratch their nose with a toe.
Turn their head to the back when resting.
Nap throughout the day.
Tuck one foot up with resting.
Grind the beak when content or before sleep.

Charli takes a well-deserved nap after chewing up a new box.

A WEEKEND DAY IN THE LIFE OF CHARLI

She sticks her head out of her Hide n' Sleep to accept a quick scritch (gentle rubbing of the feathers backward) from me when I uncover her cage. As I prepare breakfast, she slowly wakes up and comes out of her Hide 'n Sleep.

I offer her warmed oatmeal, which she loves, for breakfast. When she's had her fill she rubs her beak against the outside rim of the bowl.

Because we have more time on the weekend I take her into the shower with me instead of giving her a quick spritz from a water bottle. I place her on a special perch under the showerhead and adjust the water so that she can either move into the direct stream or stand outside it.

She invariable stands outside the direct stream so that she only gets a little wet. I don't force the issue since I want her to enjoy the water, and I know it may take many more months before she gets excited about it. Or she may never get excited about showers. I dry her off with a big fluffy towel, and place her back in her cage.

She preens. All parrots preen. A lot. She checks out her pellets and eats a few, and has a drink of water from her water bottle.

If I'm going to be working in my study, I take her into my office and settle her on her hanging gym.

There are treats at the very top of the gym to tempt her to stay put for a while. There are also numerous toys and nice big wooden things to chew.

When she finishes her treats she usually flies to my shoulder. Her wing feathers are trimmed so that she can fly but not gain altitude.

Around 11:00 it's nap time. I either put her back in her cage or let her nap on her gym, depending on how fidgety she's being.

For lunch I share some vegetables with her, which she often ignores in favor of a Nutriberri or a piece of millet.

If I don't take her out of her cage the second she thinks I should in the afternoon, she'll run back and forth in the cage to be sure I know she's there. She may climb up the side of the cage and hang upside down. There may be some chirping.

I let her come out on my finger. She'll lean forward slightly, her feathers loose and relaxed, her eyes wide. I pet her and then let her settle herself on my shoulder and "supervise" me as I open the mail and check telephone messages.

If I have to return calls I gently set her down on the coffee table (she's very jealous of the telephone), where she proceeds to investigate the books and papers, stopping every few minutes to chew one of them. I've learned from sad experience not to keep valuable books and papers scattered where Charli can find them.

If I'm doing laundry I let her supervise the sorting of the clothes (she especially enjoys chewing on the tee-shirts as they're being sorted).

When I have to be out for several hours I leave the TV on for her; I usually set the channel to PBS, though she's shown no preference for any of the networks.

She mostly naps while I am away, eats a few pellets, and preens.

When it's time for dinner I put her back in her cage; the kitchen is too dangerous with a hot stove and knives laying about.

For dinner, I give her warm vegetables and perhaps some pasta. After dinner, I let her out and we watch television together. Or at least I watch television; Charli tries to eat my couch, in between long scritching sessions.

Around 8:00 pm it's time for bed, and she's usually willing to go into her cage. I refresh her pellets and water, despite her attempts to snap at my fingers for invading her territory. I give her a treat of a Nutriberri or sometimes a piece of an almond. She'll then climb up and enter her Hide 'N Sleep. If I attempt to pet her she'll "shadow box" to warn me off. I cover her cage, and wish her sweet dreams.

Are all brown-heads like this? Of course not; each parrot is an individual, with different likes and dislikes and personalities. Your brown-head may insist on going to bed earlier, your brown-head may be afraid of the telephone or hate birdy bread. What is important is one-on-one attention and a sense of routine; not so rigid it's impossible to maintain but constant enough to depend on.

Charli always enjoys a change of scenery.

CONTINUING YOUR EDUCATION

One small book such as this cannot possibly teach you everything you need to know about brown-headed parrots.

Our knowledge of parrots has exploded in the past twenty years, and every day we learn more. It is important that you continue to keep abreast of research and findings.

While you can't believe everything you read on the Internet you can find reliable resources. One list I highly recommend is the Yahoo group Brown-Headed_Parrot.

Join a local bird club, or if your town doesn't have one, consider starting one. More people own parrots than you might think.

Attend a seminar. Take a class.

Read. To help you get started, here are some of my favorite books:

Athan, Mattie Sue, *Guide to a Well-Behaved Parrot*, 3rd edition, Barron's, Hauppauge, New York, 1999

Burgmann, Petra M., *Feeding Your Pet Bird*, Barron's, Hauppauge, New York, 1993

D'Arezzo, Carol S., and Lauren Shannon-Nunn, *Parrot Toys & Play Areas*, CrowFire Publishing, Springfield, Virginia, 2000

Doane, Bonnie Munro, *Parrot Training: A Guide to Taming and Gentling Your Avian Companion*, Howell Book House, Hoboken, New Jersey, 2001

Joron, Rick and Jean Pattison, *African Parrots*, Hancock House Publishers, Blaine, Washington, 1999

Moustaki, Nikki, *Parrots for Dummies*, Wiley Publishing, Inc., Hoboken, New Jersey, 2005

The African Brown-Headed Parrot   43

Helpful Internet Links

Brown-Headed Parrot Group on Yahoo
http://pets.groups.yahoo.com/group/brown-headed_parrots/

Listing of safe and toxic plants and branches
www.plannedparrothood.com/plants.html

Discussion boards and resources
www.upatsix.com/

African Parrot Society
www.wingscc.com/aps/

Wikipedia
http://en.wikipedia.org/wiki/Parrot

911 Parrot Alert
www.911parrotalert.com

Bird Hotline
www.hotlline.com

Charli shows off her middle-aged yellow tail feather, after chewing up my old sudoku book.

INDEX

Avian veterinarian 14-15, 16
Bathing 20, 22-23
Beak grinding 21, 38
Biting 26
Breeders 6
Breeding 35
Cages 4, 7-9, 19
Chewing 28-30, 38
Children 5, 27
Cleaning 9-10
Contact calls 26
Dangers 5
Description 1
Diet 16-18, 37
Escape 35-36
Foods 17-18, 37
Foraging 30-31
Grooming 22-23
Health and illness 14-16
Invisibility 32
Jealousy 27
Molting 19-20, 38
Night frights 31
Nails 22
Perches 7-8, 10, 19
Play 12, 33-34
Poop 15, 18-19
Preening 25, 38
Quarantine 11-12
Regurgitation 33
Screaming 21, 26
Sleep 16, 19, 38
Sounds 21
Step-ups 24
Talking 21
Treats 18
Weaning 7
Well-bird exam 14
Wing trimming 23

www.ingramcontent.com/pod-product-compliance
Lightning Source LLC
Chambersburg PA
CBHW072038060426
42449CB00010BA/2337